Cinderella

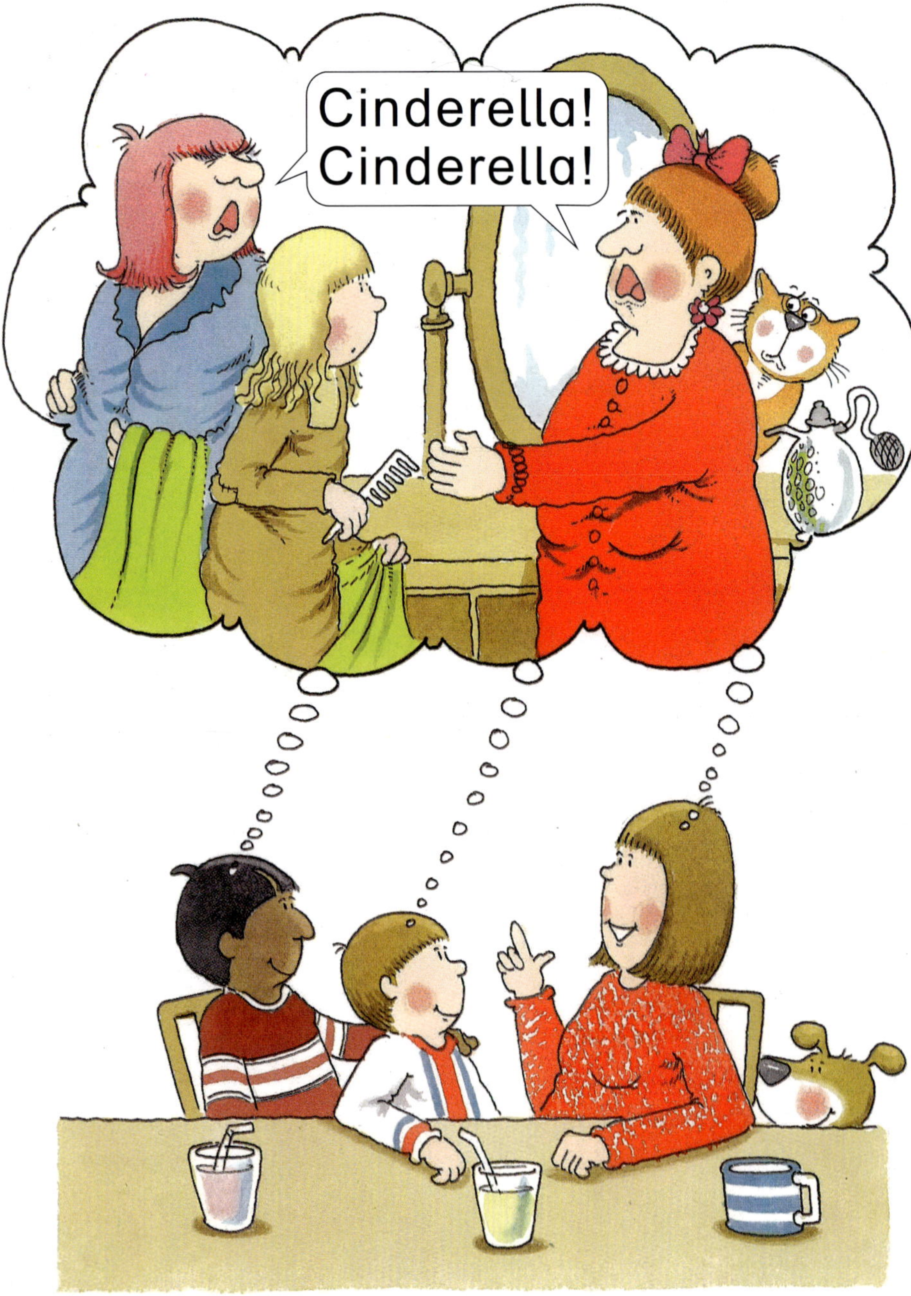
Cinderella!
Cinderella!

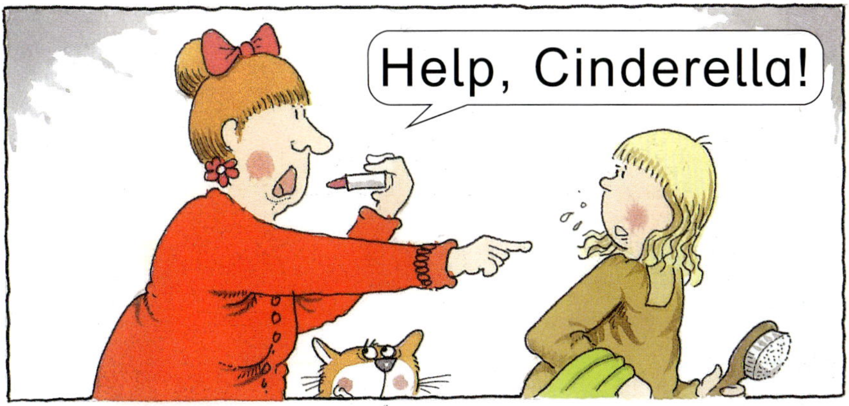
Help, Cinderella!

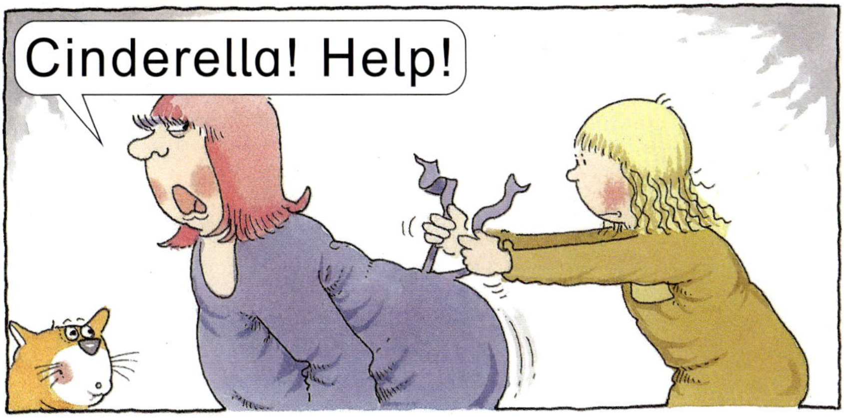
Cinderella! Help!

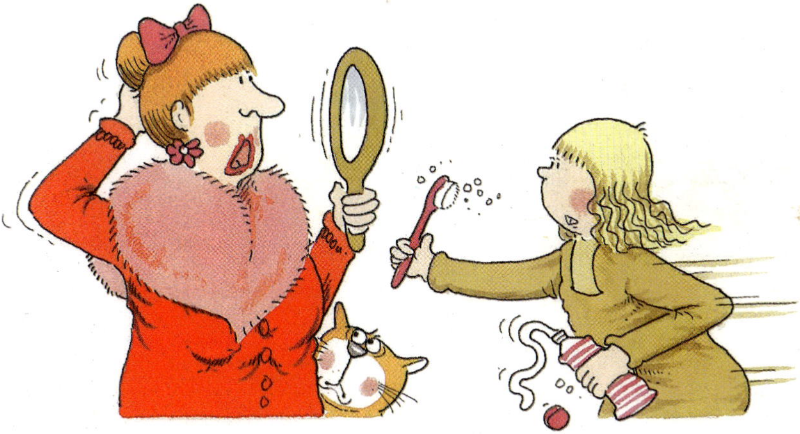

Cinderella helps.

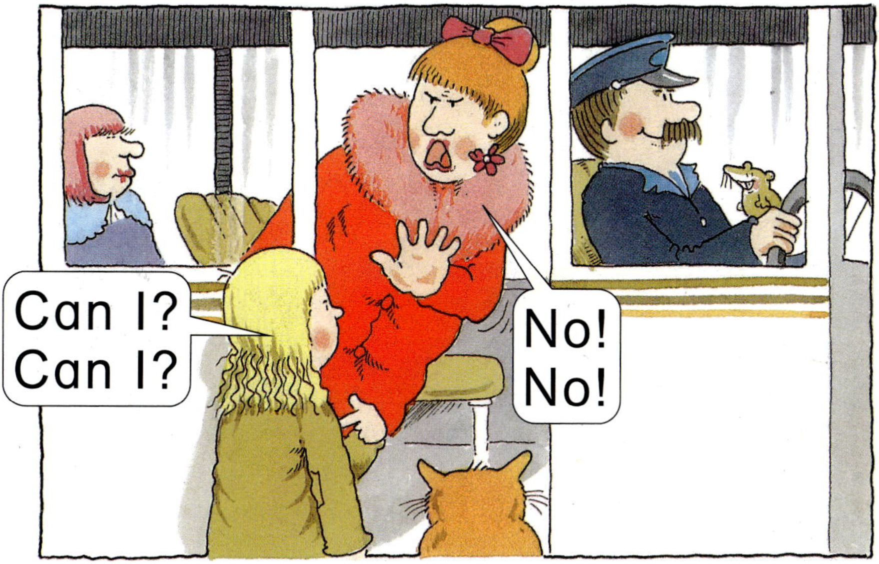
Can I?
Can I?
No!
No!

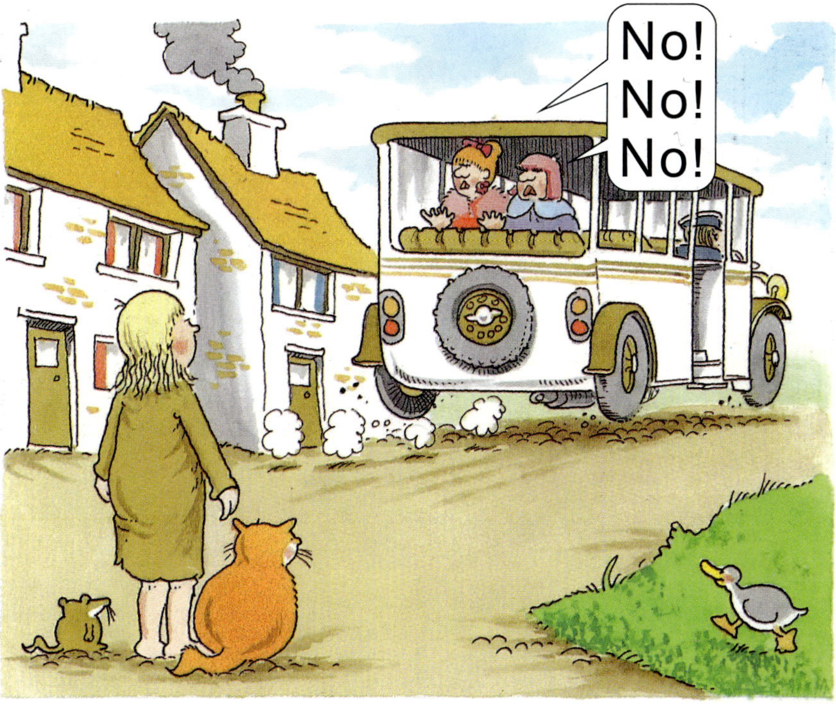
No!
No!
No!

Cinderella went down.

Down,
down,

down went Cinderella.

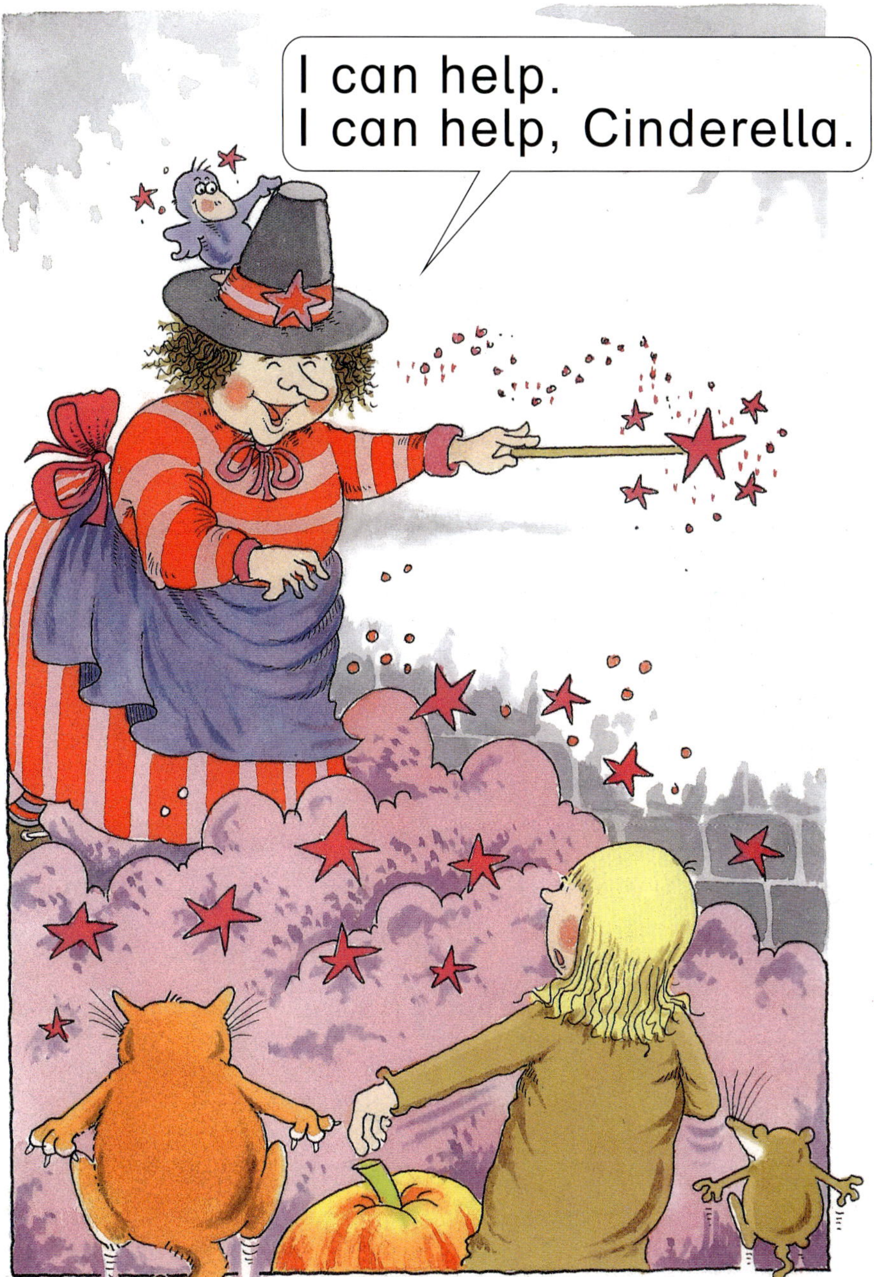
I can help.
I can help, Cinderella.

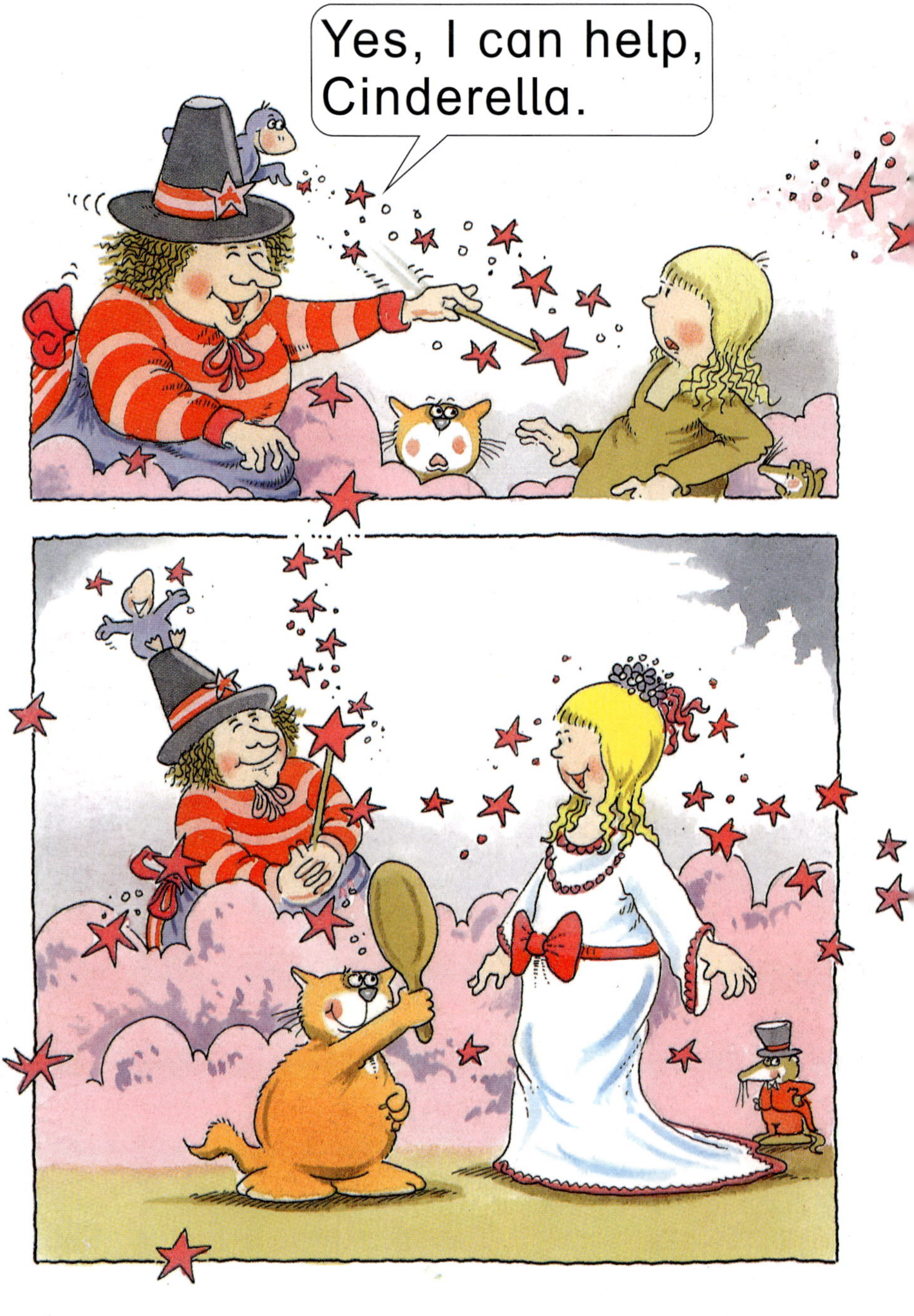
Yes, I can help,
Cinderella.

Cinderella likes it!

Cinderella ran up.

Cinderella went in.

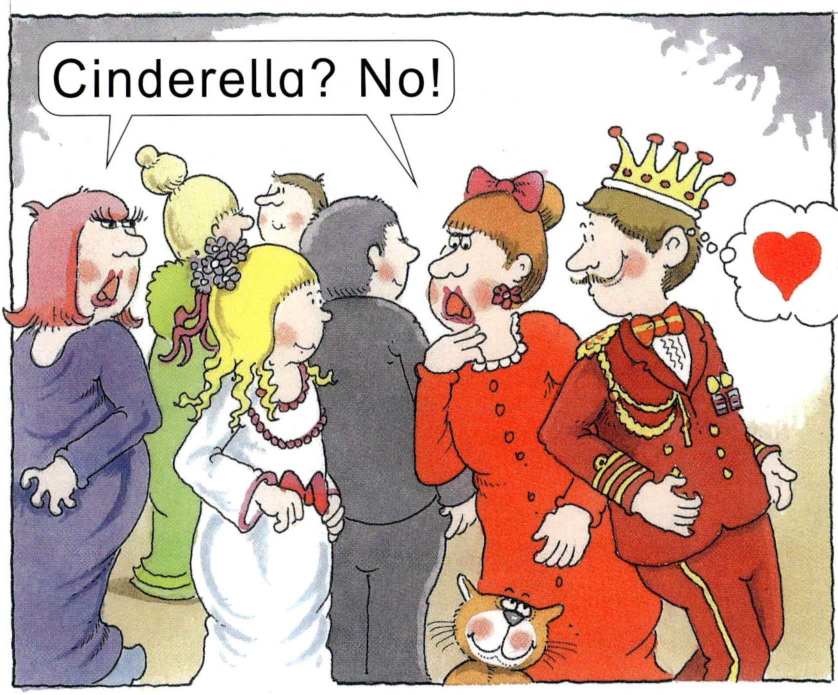
Cinderella? No!

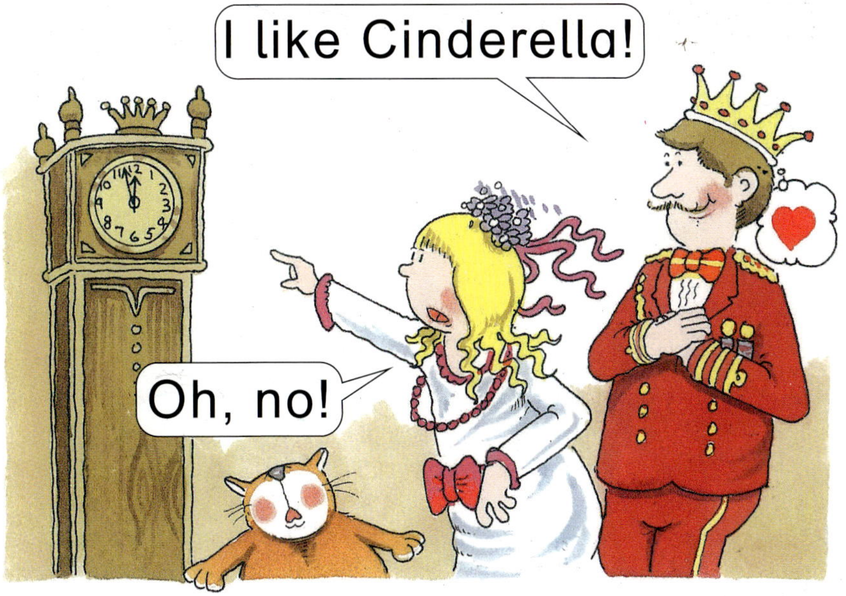
I like Cinderella!
Oh, no!

Cinderella ran down.

Down,

down,

down ran Cinderella.

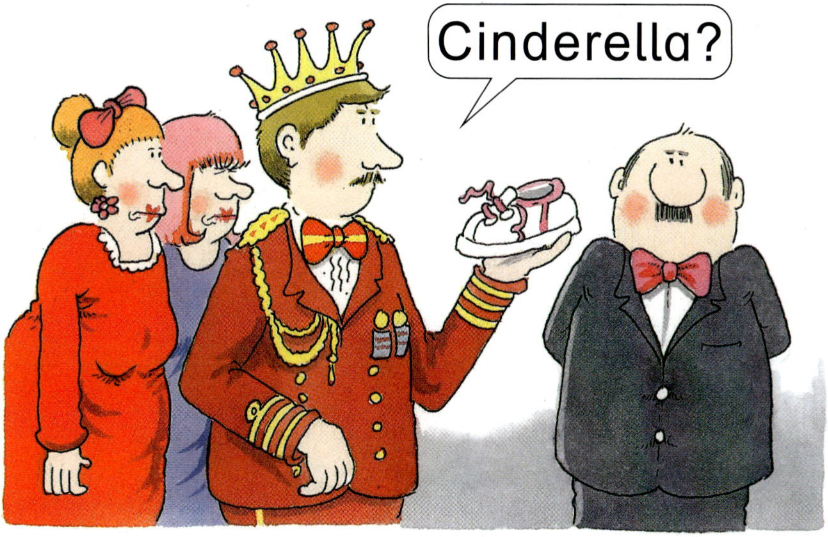
Cinderella?

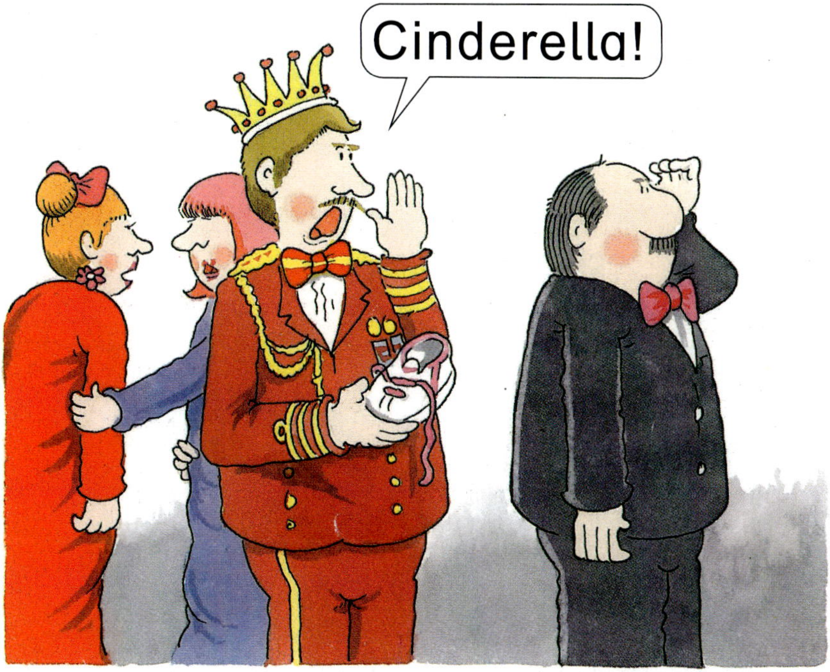
Cinderella!

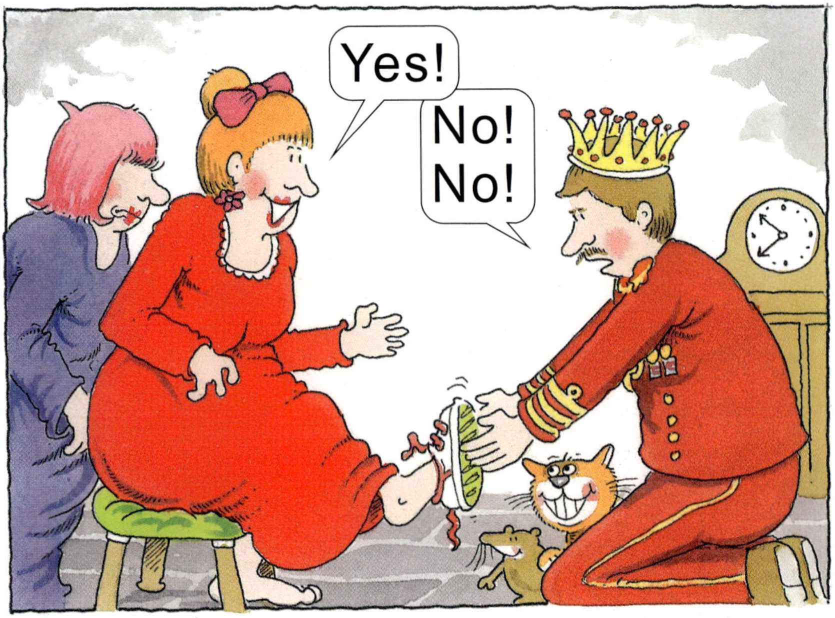
Yes!
No!
No!

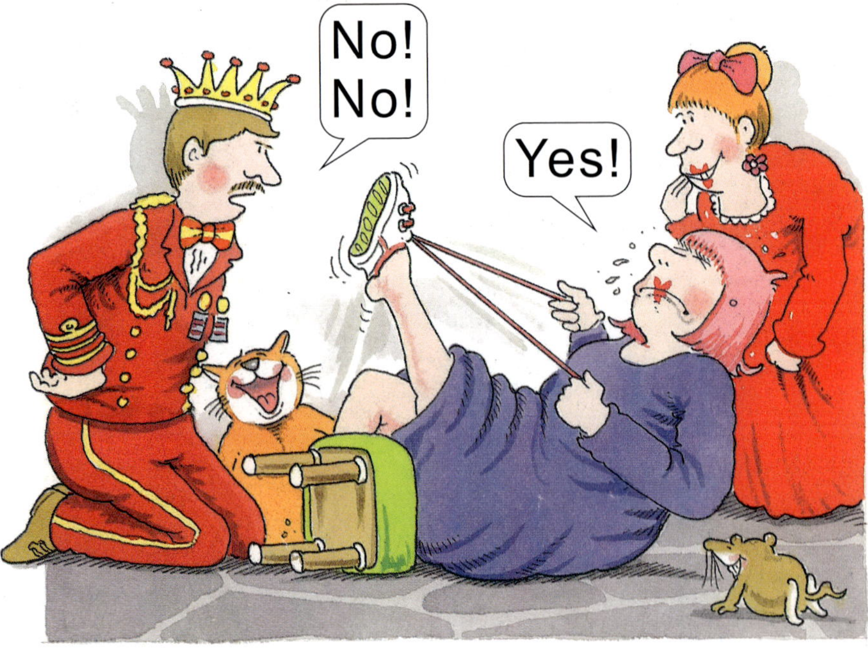
No!
No!
Yes!

Down he
went to
Cinderella.

Yes! It is Cinderella!